David Collins

GUIDELINES ON Figured Bass

with exercises

Grades 6-8

Eric McDonald
Chan-Chiu Lu Yah

© RHYTHM MP SDN. BHD. 1994

Sole Distributor:
RHYTHM MP SDN. BHD.
2060 & 2061, Jalan Persekutuan, Permatang Tinggi Light Industry,
14000 Seberang Perai Tengah,
Penang, Malaysia.
Tel: 04-5873689 (Direct Line), 04-5873690 (Hunting Line)
Fax: 04-5873691
E-mail: rhythm_mp@mphsb.po.my

Published by
RHYTHM MP SDN. BHD.

Cover Design & Pre-press by
CP TECH SDN. BHD.

Printed in Malaysia by
MONOSETIA SDN. BHD.

ISBN 967-985-435-3
Order No.: MPG-4008

Contents

Figured Bass
Grade 6

Harmonizing a figured bass.

For this grade the requirements are:

(1) How to write and use chords in root position.

(2) First and second inversion chords on all degress of the major and minor scales.

(3) V_7 in all inversions.

(4) II_7 in root position and first inversion.

This system was developed during the Baroque period 1600-1750.

It enables musicians to read and play chords from the numbers above the bass notes i.e. a kind of musical shorthand. It is rather like the chord symbols used be guitarists or keyboard players in pop music.

The numbers under the bass represent intervals above the bass that will form the notes of the chord. The system deals only with the intervals above the bass and not with the roots of the chords.

The following table shows how the symbols are used for root position, first and second inversion and seventh chords and their inversions.

		Complete figured bass symbol	Symbol most often used
DIATONIC CHORDS	root position	$\begin{matrix}5\\3\end{matrix}$	–
	first inversion	$\begin{matrix}6\\3\end{matrix}$	6
	second inversion	$\begin{matrix}6\\4\end{matrix}$	$\begin{matrix}6\\4\end{matrix}$
SEVENTH CHORDS	root position	$\begin{matrix}7\\5\\3\end{matrix}$	7
	first inversion	$\begin{matrix}6\\5\\3\end{matrix}$	$\begin{matrix}6\\5\end{matrix}$
	second inversion	$\begin{matrix}6\\4\\3\end{matrix}$	$\begin{matrix}4\\3\end{matrix}$
	third inversion	$\begin{matrix}6\\4\\2\end{matrix}$	$\begin{matrix}4\\2\end{matrix}$

(1) A missing symbol represents a root position chord.

(2) 6 represents a first inversion major or minor chord depending on the key-signature.

(3) An accidental next to a number indicates a raising or lowering of that interval. E.g.:

(4) An accidental on its own always refers to the third above the bass that is being altered.

Example

Look at the following example of a figured bass followed by a possible interpretation that might be played by a continuo player in Bach's time.

Working Method

Harmonizing a figured bass.

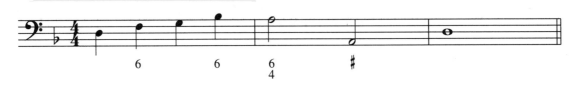

Step 1

Add Roman letters to the figures.

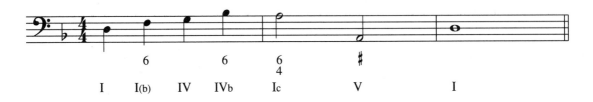

Step 2

(a) Decide on the cadence point.

(b) Begin the soprano line at the cadence and the approach chord to the cadence.

Suggest a common note on IVb-Ic and resolve leading to the tonic.

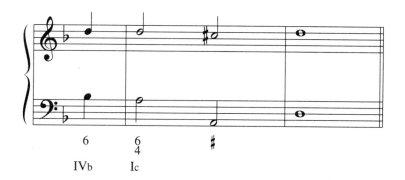

Note:

i)   The tonic is a safe note to double.

ii) Avoid doubling the third in a major chord.

iii) The leading note should always resolve to the tonic.

iv) The 7th of the V_7 should resolve downwards to the 3rd degree of the key.

v)   The inner parts should progress to the nearest possible intervals.

vi) Try to have the highest part move in contrary motion to the bass.

Step 3

Complete the melody line.

(a) Suggest to start with the 3rd of the chord for the top voice, progress down in inversion to the bass.

(b) Continue the pattern downwards.

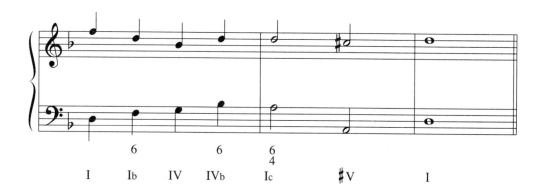

Note:

When writing the top voice, always avoid:

i)   Augmented intervals.

ii) Consecutive 5ths or 8^{ve}.

iii) Doubling the 3rd of the chord or leading note.

7

Step 4

Write the inner parts.

(a) Do the alto and tenor parts simultaneously.

Keep the inner parts moving as close as possible because the melody and bass are fairly active.

(b) Complete the cadence first.

The tenor will need to double the tonic leaving the 3rd for the alto.

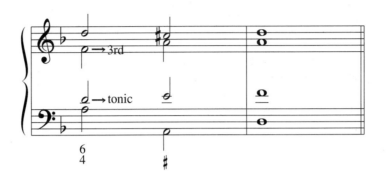

(c) Next complete the approach chord IVb.

The tenor should keep the common note and the alto gets the tonic.

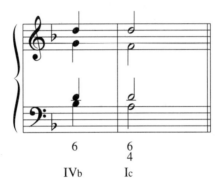

(d) Complete the remaining chords.

Check for mistakes.

Some common chord progressions

(1) At cadence points.

    II7b   Ic   V7   I

II7b is more suitable in this cadential pattern.

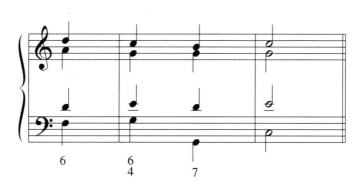

Note:

(a) The tonic is doubled on the first chord.

(b) Avoid doubling the 3rd of any of the chords.

(2) Passing 6/4.

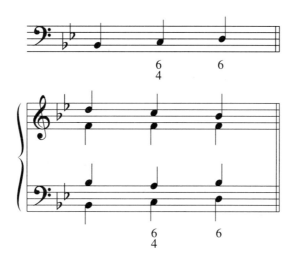

Note:

(a) The melody is the same as the bass but in reverse order.

(b) Alto is having the common note.

(c) Tenor moves from tonic - leading note - tonic.

(3) Resolution of V₇ in all inversions.

In root position:

(a) The leading note must rise to the tonic and the 7th of the V₇ falls to the 3rd of chord I.

(b) Do not double the 7th of the V₇ or the leading note.

(c) The 5th of the V₇ can be omitted.

In root position

(a)   (b)   (c)

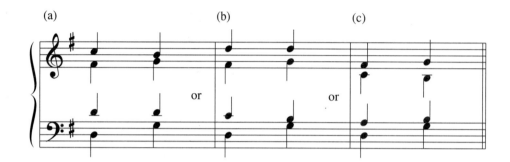

Note that at:

(a) The 5th is omitted.

(b) The 3rd is doubled at the unison.

In 1st inversion

(a)   (b)   (c)

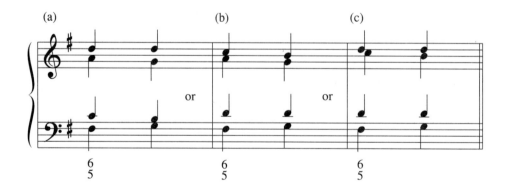

Note that the 5th is missing in (c).

Used as a passing 6/4.

In 2nd inversion

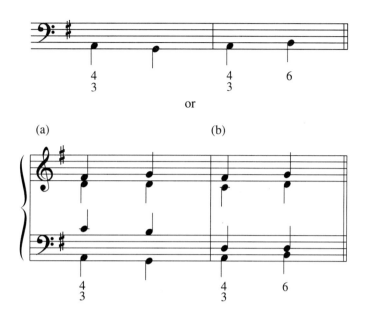

In example (b) the 7th must resolve upwards to avoid doubling the 3rd.

In 3rd inversion

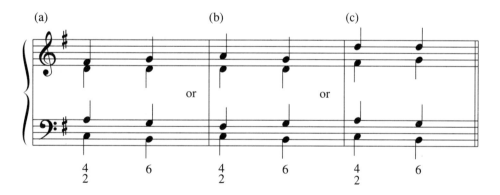

The bass, being the 7th of the chord will have to resolve downwards by step.

Exercises

Harmonize these figured basses.

(1)

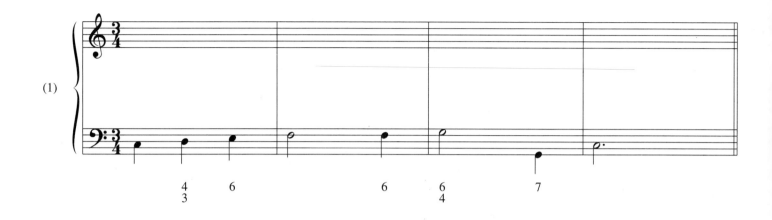

(2)

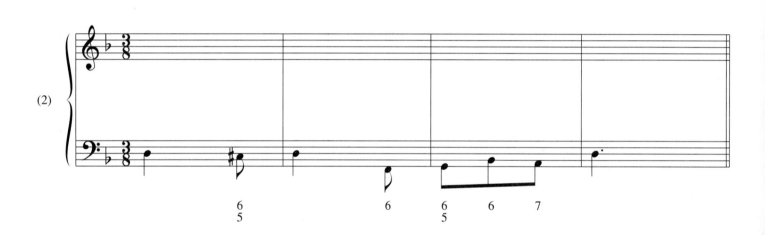

(3)

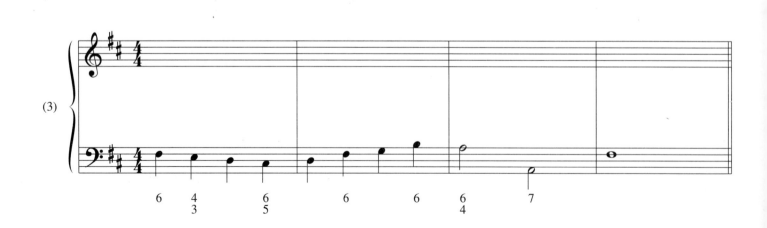

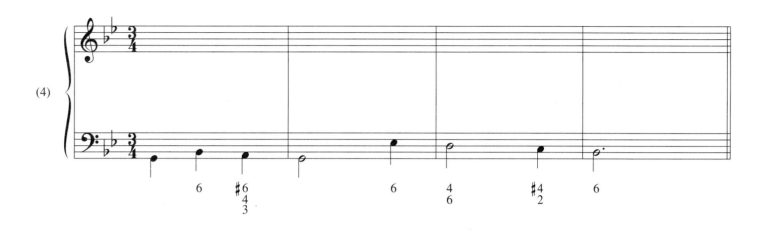

(4)

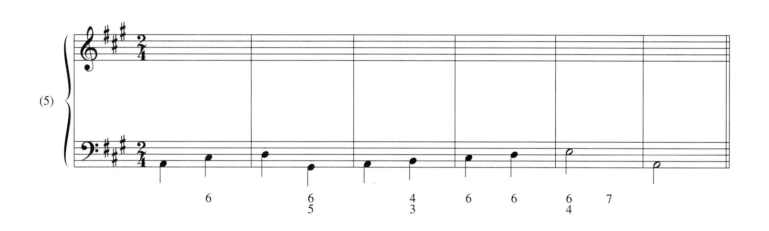

(5)

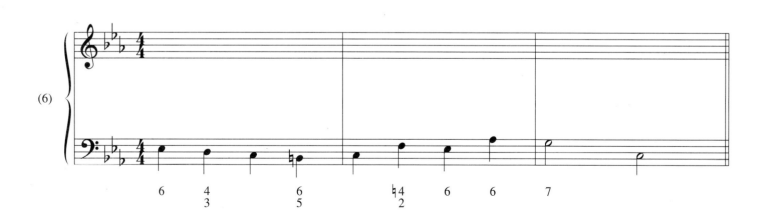

(6)

13

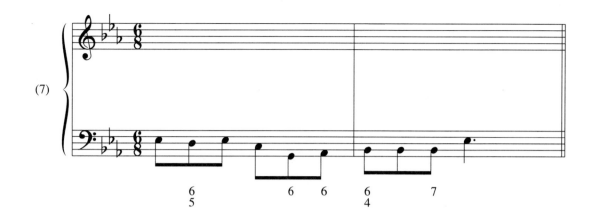

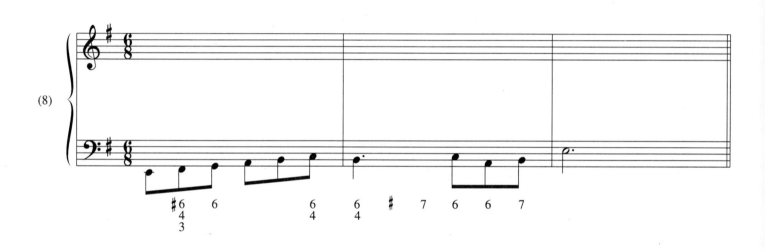

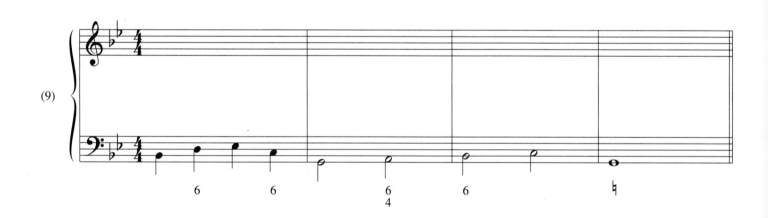

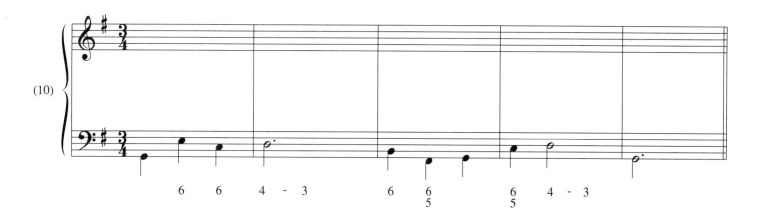

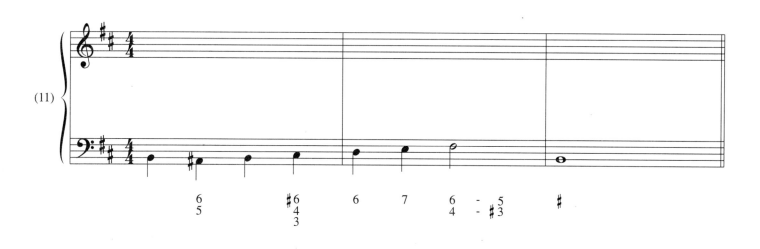

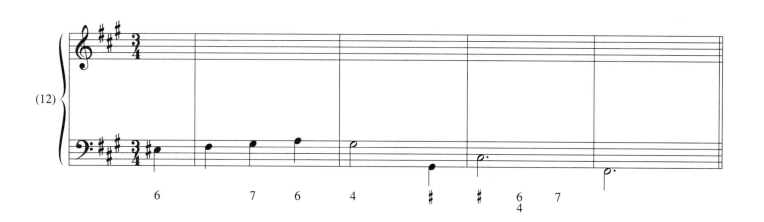

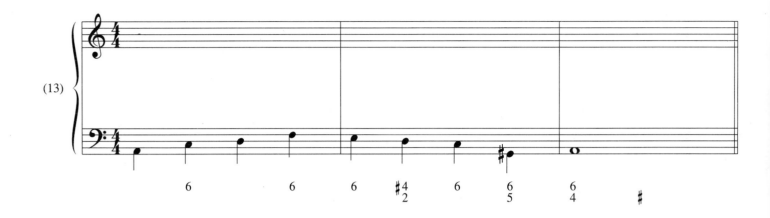

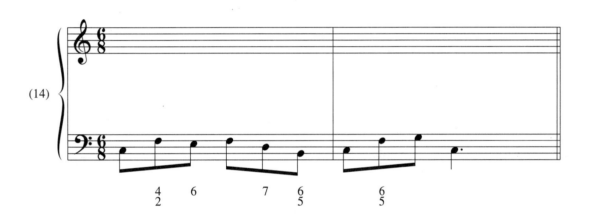

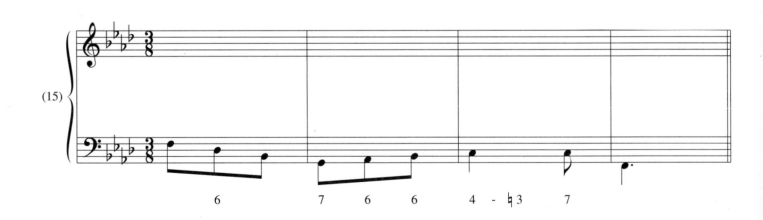

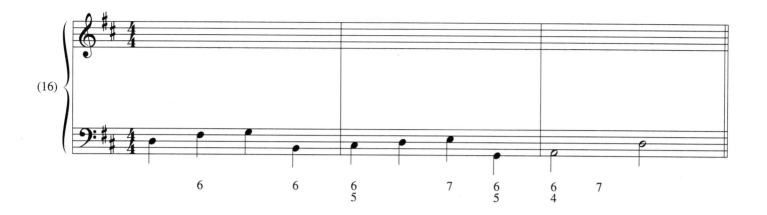

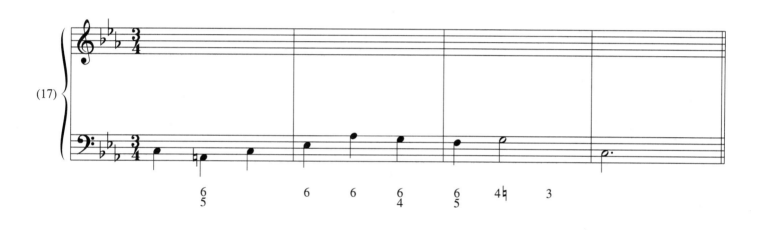

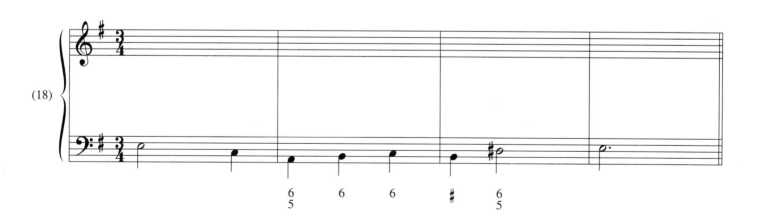

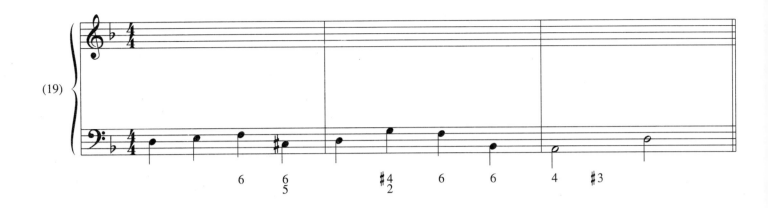

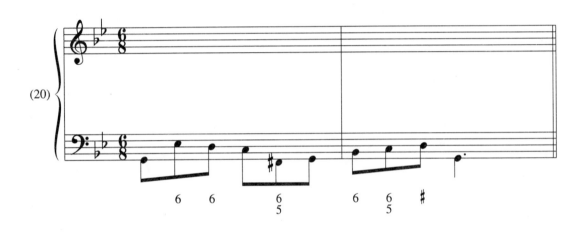

Grade 7

In this grade:

(1) For this question you will be given a two-part extract in the Baroque style. The bass will be figured for the first few bars. You are required to continue the harmony by figuring the bass.

(2) All chords have to be figured except for root position chords.

(3) Suspensions are common and these need to be indicated.

(4) Knowledge of V_7 and II_7, their inversions and resolutions is required.

Suspensions

A suspension is a chord note that is being held whilst the other parts move on.

A suspension is identified by a 3 stage pattern.

(1) Preparation

The preparation is the chord before the suspension which contains a note which is either sustained tied or repeated.

(2) Suspension

The suspended note is sustained tied or repeated. In most cases it is a non-harmony note.

(3) Resolution

The resolution is effected when the suspended note falls one step to become the harmony note of the resolution chord.

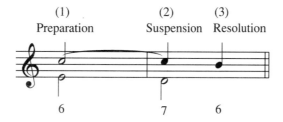

The suspension is figured according to the interval from the bass.

The note of resolution should not be doubled, except 9-8.

Some common suspensions:

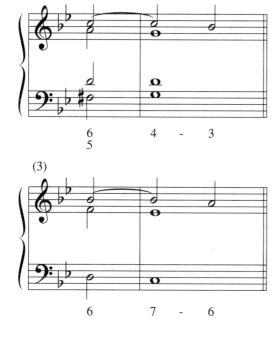

If the bass moves to a different note on the resolution chord with the suspended upper voice, we have a suspension with a change of bass.

Example 1

Working Method

Indicate suitable chords for a continuo player by figuring the bass from bar 5 onwards. All chords except root position (5/3) should be shown. Suspended dissonances should also be indicated.

In the following example, the passage ends in the dominant - A major.

Preludio from Sonata no.8

Step 1

Identify all the cadences.

(a) As the extract ends on the dominant, the harmony would definitely require a Perfect cadence in A major at bars 11-12.

(b) At bars 4-5 the bass implies an imperfect cadence.

(c) Consider the approach chords to the cadence.

    Remember that II or II₇ or Ic often precede V.

    At bars 11-12 the only possibility would be Ic.

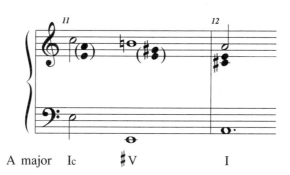

The approach chord to IVb at bar 4 can only be I because of the Vb at the last chord of bar 3. So no figure is required.

Step 2

Check for any passing modulations. These are very common in this style and are usually approached by a secondary dominant.

At bars 5-6, the descending bass pattern G-F, suggests a V₇d-Ib, with a 7-6 suspension in the soprano.

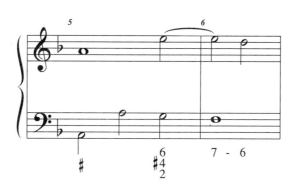

The same occurs at bars 7-8 but the key suggested here is A minor.

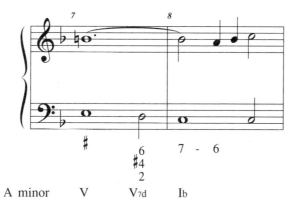

Step 3

Analyse the remaining bars 9-10.

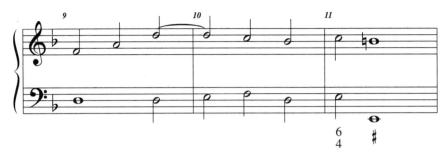

(a) The broken chord in the melody strongly suggest a D minor in root position.

(b) At bar 10, the tied D in the soprano suggest a suspension. The resolution includes a change of bass.

(c) The repeated Es at bar 11 indicate an E major chord, the dominant preparation for A major at bar 12.

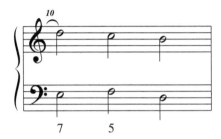

(d) The next chord strongly suggest II$_{(7)}$ as an approach chord to the 6/4 5/3 cadence.

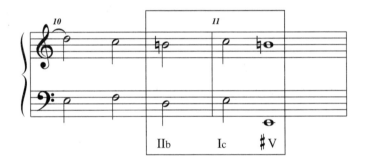

Step 4

The completed exercise.

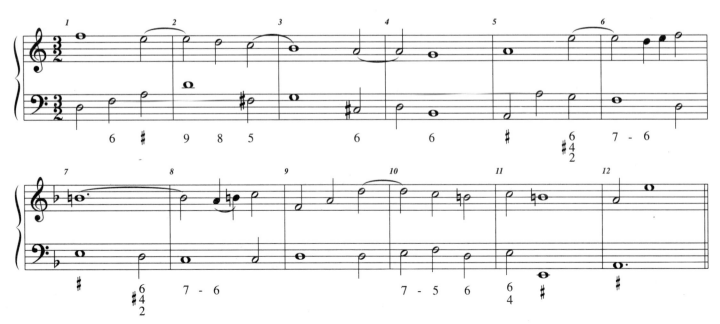

Working Method

Example 2

Indicate suitable chords for a continuo player by figuring the bass from bar 5 onwards. All chords except root position should be shown. Suspended dissonances should also be indicated.

Sonata VIII

Step 1

Identify all the cadences.

(i) This extract ends with a perfect cadence in the tonic key with a $\frac{6}{4}$ - $\frac{5}{4}$ - $_3$ suspension.

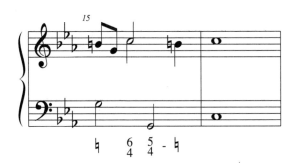

(ii) Bars 7-8 indicates a sequence of bars 3-4 with a phrygian cadence (IVb →V) in G minor.

Step 2

Check for passing modulations.

The chromatic passages at 9-10 and 12-14 suggest passing modulations.

(i) Smooth voice leading can be achieved by including a 7th chord on each passing chord ∗. The pattern implies a cycle of 5ths.

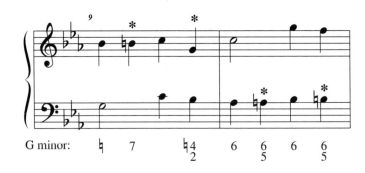

(ii) This pattern is also good for bars 12-14.

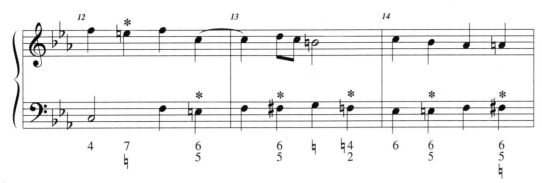

Note: The F-E♮ over the C bass indicates a 4-3 suspension.

Step 3

Analyse the remaining bars.

(i) Bars 5-6 show an exact sequence of bars 1-2. The key is G minor.
Simply repeat the figures.

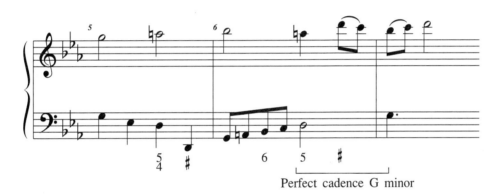

(ii) Bar 11

Last beat of bar 10 ($\frac{6}{5}$ chord) indicates dominant 7th approach to C minor at beat one of bar 11. Beat 2 shows a passing modulation.

Beat 4 indicates 1st inversion of $V_{7(b)}$-I in C minor with a 4-3 suspension in the passing.

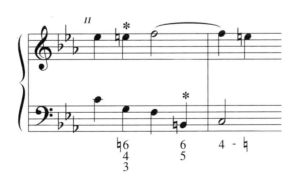

Step 4

The completed exercise.

Grave

Exercises

Indicate suitable chords for a continuo player by figuring the bass in the following passage. 5/3 chords need not be shown, but all other chords should be indicated, as should any suspended dissonances.

(1)

ARIA

Bach Cantata

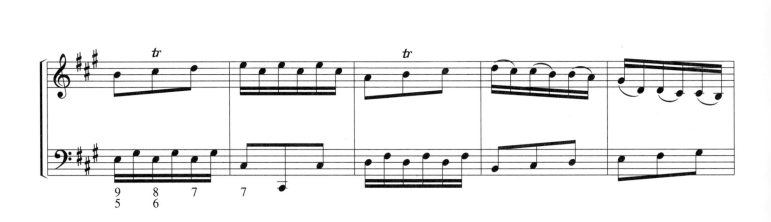

(3)

ARIA

(4)

ARIE (Duett.)

(5)

ARIA

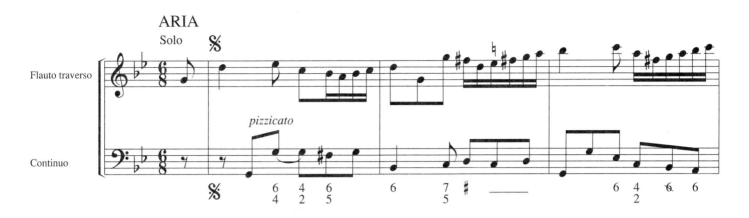

Grade 7

(6)

ARIE

Grade 8

In this grade:

(1) The opening of a Trio Sonata movement is given. The bass is fully figured.

(2) You are required to complete the two violin parts of which only the opening is given.

(3) The piece will be in the imitative style typical of the period.

(4) The writing will need to conform to the harmony indicated by the bass figuration.

(5) You will need to identify suspensions, cadences and phrasing.

(6) There may be frequent use of passing modulations.

Example

Complete the violin parts in the following passage from a trio sonata movement by Corelli following the figuring as shown under the basso continuo.

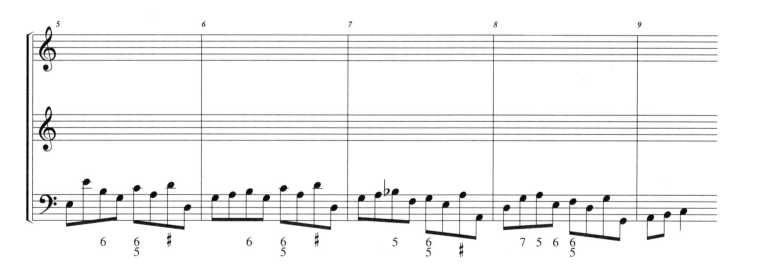

Step 1

Sketch the harmony of the continuo part, checking for cadences, repetitions and sequences.

The upbeat to each bar contains a V-I sequence in various keys.

Bars 1-2   C major
    2-3   C major
    3-4   E minor
    4-5   E minor
    5-6   G major
    6-7   G minor
    7-8   D minor
    8-9   A minor (interrupted cadence)

Step 2

Identify cadences.

(a) The repeated E minor cadence at bars 4 and 5 implies an important cadence and the end of the first phrase.

(b) The interrupted cadence at bars 8-9 marks the end of the second phrase.

Step 3

Analyse the Violin parts.

Look at both the melody and the rhythm of the given part.

The Violin has two distinct musical ideas.

(a) Melodically, there is a upward movement by step followed by a downward leap.

(b) Rhythmically it can be broken down to 2 ideas:

Step 4

Working out the parts.

(a) Check for repetitions.

The beginning of the second phrase can be a transposed repeat of the first phrase for both violins in E minor.

(b) Fill in the cadences.

   (i)   Perfect cadence at bars 4-5.

       Violin I must take the E because of the D♯ leading note at the last beat of bar 4.

   (ii) Interrupted cadence at bars 8-9.

       The rhythm of the opening of Violin I would be suitable.

       Violin II moves from a suspension to the 3rd of the chord.

In bar 8, the 6 is in Violin II, so tie it over. Violin I will need to take the 7 and 5 as it makes a strong descending step pattern (F E D C).

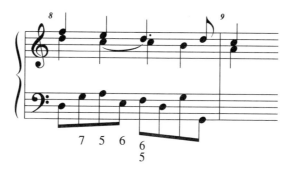

Step 5

Complete the remaining bars.

(a) At bar 4 the D♯ leading note in Violin I must resolve to E and then carry on to F♯ leading to G in bar 5. This gives a good approach to the cadence at bar 5.

Violin II: The F♯ must rise to G causing an overlapping of parts. This is however acceptable. The figures will require Violin II to take these notes.

Add interest by:

(i)   Turn the repeated Es into a tied note giving a suspension with Violin I.

(ii) Adding the rhythm of the second motif to the first beat.

Bars 5 and 6 are covered (see step 4).

(b) At bar 7:

Violin I must take G because of the F♯ at the last beat of bar 6. It then goes on to F♮ to satisfy the B♭(5) in the figured bass, followed by a step down to the E of the next chord.

Violin II: The A will ascend well to B♭ at bar 7, being the 3rd of the G minor chord. A leap down to D will be necessary to allow the 3rd of the next chord to suspend at the 6/5♯ figure. This will then resolve on the C♯ at the last beat of bar 7.

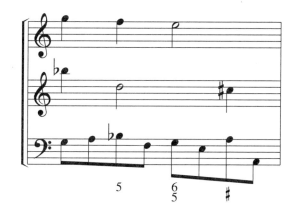

Checking with bar 8, a sequence can be written in Violin I by adjusting the rhythm, thus:

(c) Violin II: A sequence can be maintained in Violin II.

37

Step 6

The complete working.

Allegro

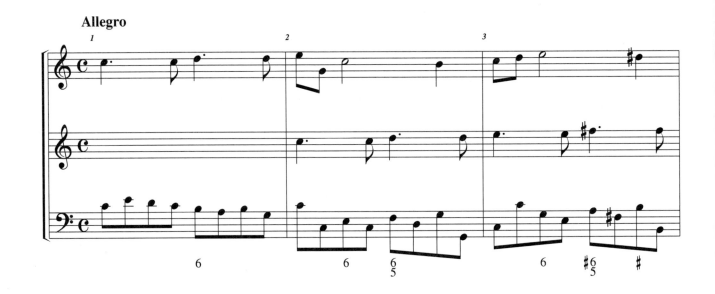

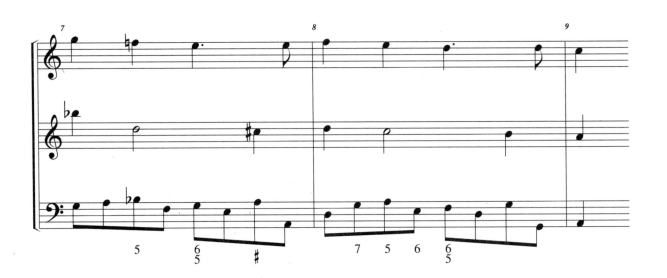

Exercises

Complete the violin parts in the following passages from a trio sonata movement, following the figuring shown under the basso continuo.

(1)

Sonata I

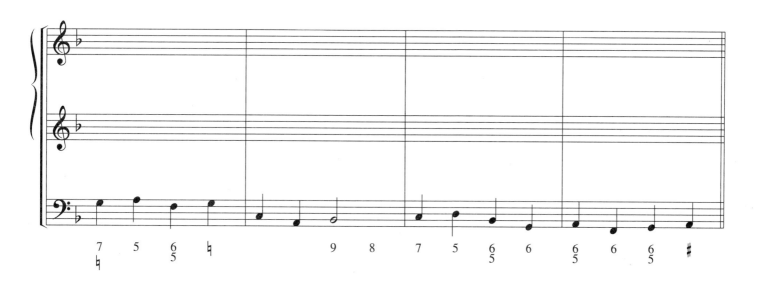

Sonata VIII

Corelli

Vivace

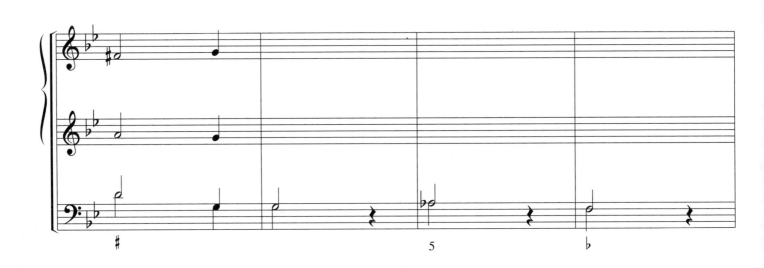

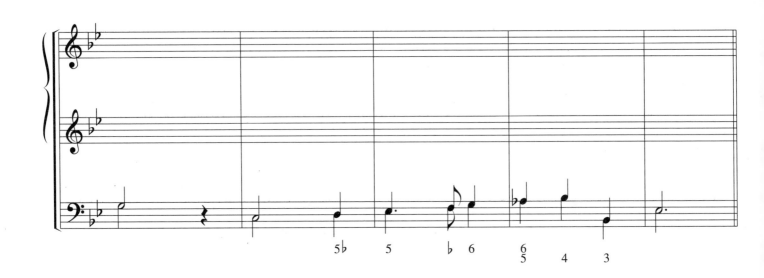

Sonata VI

Corelli

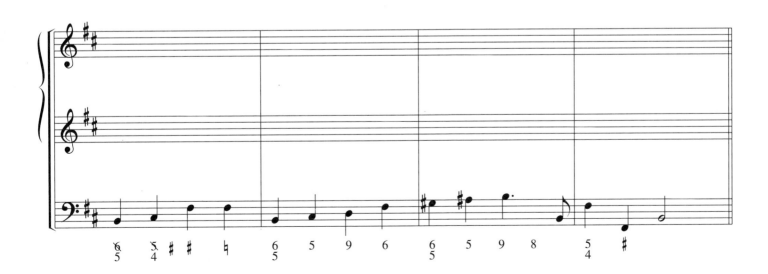

Sonata X
Preludio

Sonata VIII

Grave

Corelli

Violino I

Violino II

Violone
o Arcileuto
Organo

Grade 8

Sonata XII

Corelli

Grave

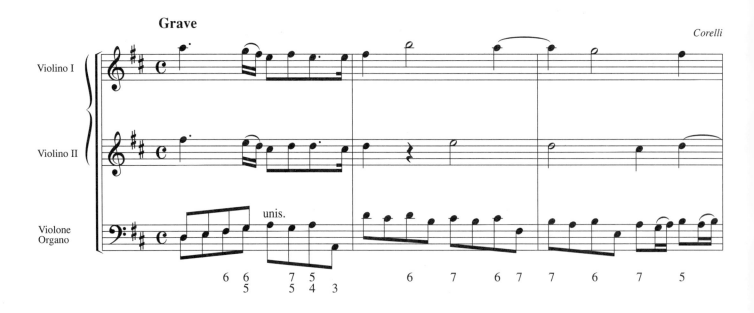

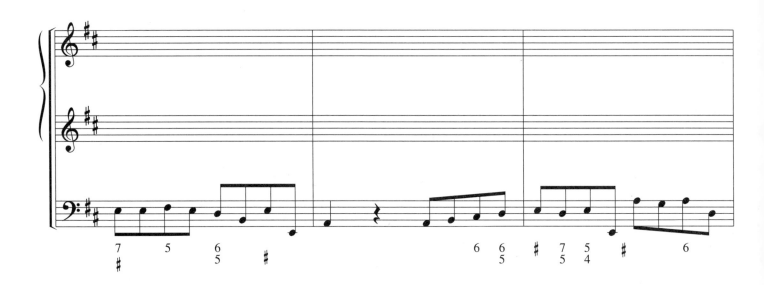

Sonata XI

Corelli

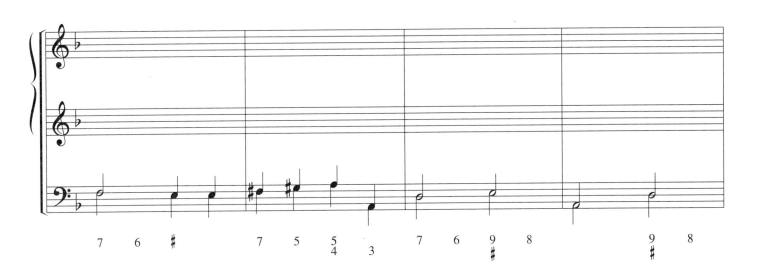

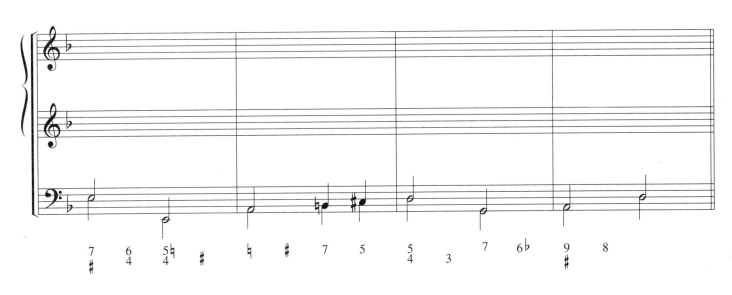

Grade 8

Sonata I

Preludio

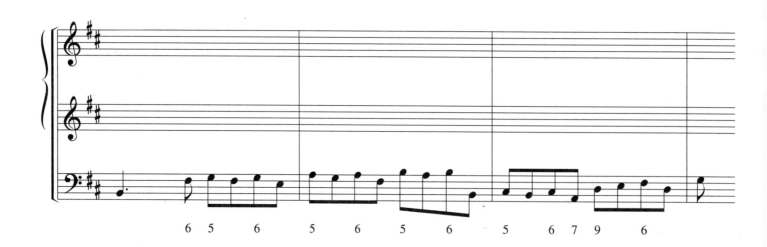